DATE			

▲▲▲▲▲▲▲▲▲▲▲▲

HATS
are for
WATERING
HORSES

WHY THE COWBOY DRESSED THAT WAY

▼

Hats are for Watering Horses
Why the Cowboy Dressed That Way

by Mary Blount Christian

Illustrated by Lyle Miller

Hendrick-Long Publishing Co.

To my son, Scott

Library of Congress Cataloging-in-Publication Data

Christian, Mary Blount.
    Hats are for watering horses : why the cowboy dressed that way / by
Mary Blount Christian ; illustrated by Lyle Miller.
        p.   cm.
    ISBN 0-937460-89-3. — ISBN 0-937460-95-8 (pc)
    1. Cowboys—West (U.S.)—Costume—Juvenile literature.
[1. Cowboys—Costume.]   I. Miller, Lyle   ill.   II. Title.
F596.C373   1994
391'.04636—dc20   —dc20
[973.7'1]

                                                                93-35748
                                                                    CIP
                                                                     AC

Book design: Flying Colors Studio

Hendrick-Long Publishing Co.
Dallas, Texas 75225-1123

CONTENTS

▲▲▲▲▲▲▲▲▲▲▲

PREFACE

Why the Cowboy Dressed That Way

Just about everything a cowboy needed for his survival he wore. From head to toe his clothing was functional. He did not wear white if he was good, or black if he was bad. And he never strutted about in rhinestone-studded splendor.

The cowboy's life was a rugged routine. He was hard-working and poorly paid, and the clothes he wore were as important to him as his horse. Without his bandanna he might have choked on the dust or been blinded by the sun. And many a time, his pointy-toed, high-heeled boots saved him from being thrown from his horse and trampled to death by cattle.

HATS ARE FOR WATERING HORSES describes the cowboy's few possessions and explains that what he owned he wore and treasured. And as flamboyant as his dress may seem to us today, every bit of it was absolutely essential. With charming simplicity, author Mary Blount Christian explains the "whys" behind every stitch, buckle, and loop, so that we learn about cowboys from head to toe. And though some people may continue to debate whether or not clothes make the man, Ms. Christian makes one thing clear—hats are for watering horses.

▼

1

THE COWBOY

The sun was as hot as a branding iron.
No breeze rippled a blade of prairie grass.

The cattle stumbled blindly forward
to the urgings of the cowboy.
"Git on! Whoop! Whoop!" he called.

▲▲▲▲▲▲▲▲▲▲▲

He pulled his kerchief over his nose
as a thousand hooves kicked dust in his face.

Suddenly the nostrils of the lead steer flared.
He lifted his head and bellowed loudly.

Quickly the cowboy braced himself in the saddle
and spurred his horse.

The thirsty steer had smelled water ahead.
Breaking from the herd, he raced toward the water.
The others followed in a frenzy.

▲▲▲▲▲▲▲▲▲▲▲

To the front of the herd the cowboy galloped.
At last he caught up to the lead steer.

The cowboy twirled his lariat once, twice,
then over the head of the frantic animal.

Slowly, gently, he slowed him to a trot.
The others slowed, too.

The panicked steers might have trampled each other
to reach the water.
But now they drank peacefully from the stream.

▲▲▲▲▲▲▲▲▲▲▲

For a dollar a day and sourdough biscuits and beans
the cowboy protected the cattle from starvation,
weather, rustlers, and each other.

He wore his wide-brimmed hat
and his high-heeled boots with pride.
For they told all who saw him that he was a cowboy.
And they were as practical as they were colorful.

From head to toe the cowboy dressed
not just for comfort, or even for convenience.
He dressed to save his life.

2

▲▲▲▲▲▲▲▲▲▲▲

THE HAT

Even in town the cowboy wore his working clothes.
In each store window he saw the reflection
of his ten-gallon hat.

He knew he made a dandy picture.
And everyone recognized him by his headgear.

The width of his brim and even the peak and crease
of his crown told what part of the country he was from.

A more narrow brim and a lower crown
that was creased all around
was used by the northern cowboy.
But the southern cowboy needed a wider brim
and a higher crown for more protection.

To the cowboy his hat was more than a head cover.
It was his way of life.

He spent a month's wages or more on his wide-brimmed
hat at the general store.
Then he banded it with beads, braided metal wires,
or even a rattlesnake skin.
His hat was as personal as his signature.

It was his shade from the searing sun.
And it was his umbrella against drenching rains.

The high dome helped cool his head.
And a front crease helped shed water.

On the range the cowboy found many uses for his hat.

It didn't really hold ten gallons
as its nickname suggested.
But its dome was a handy trough for watering horses!

And it made a dandy feed bag
when it was filled with oats.

If the cowboy was thirsty, he merely turned up the brim
and dipped his hat into a running stream.

During a roundup he might use his hat
to whack a slow steer.
Or he might use it to signal a distant rider-
there was no need to ride that long distance!

When he wanted to wash up at chowtime,
he used his hat for an instant washbasin.
He waved his hat over the embers to fan them
into a crackling fire.
And when he was finished he simply doused the fire
with water from his hat.

At night his hat became his pillow.
And sometimes it was used to show bravery.

"Slim," someone might drawl over the evening campfire,
"I bet you can't ride that new bronc
without grabbing leather."

Quick to take a dare, the cowboy would forget
his aching muscles.
Grabbing his hat, he would head for the bronc.
While the others cheered him (or the horse),
he would mount up.

With the reins in his left hand,
he held his hat high in the air with his right hand.

No one could accuse him of grabbing leather
(holding onto the saddle)
when he waved his banner so proudly with his free hand.

▲▲▲▲▲▲▲▲▲▲▲

Before the western hat, cowboys used the sombrero
of the Mexican gauchos.
But John B. Stetson, an easterner, rode west.
A hat designer and feltmaker, he saw the need for a hat
as unique and functional as the one who would wear it.
So he made the first "cowboy" hat.

The hat became worn and stained.
And it lost its original shape.
But the cowboy would have sooner given up his ration
of sourdough and beans than to surrender his hat.

3

▲▲▲▲▲▲▲▲▲▲

THE BANDANNA

Weather was no friend to the cowboy.
In the summer the scorching sun
blistered and tormented him.
In the winter the sleet pelted him,
and the blinding snow spread in every direction.

A small square cloth seems an unlikely protection
against such odds.
But the cowboy's bandanna offered him both comfort
and protection.

He called it his "wipes."
Most of the time it was knotted at the back
and hung loosely over his chest.
But the bandanna had many uses.

Rustlers and bandits sometimes
hid their identities behind a bandanna mask.
The cowboy often wore his wipes over his face, too.
But his reason for doing so
was different from the outlaws'.
Riding drag behind a herd of cattle,
he might have chocked on the dust.
But he filtered out the dust with his bandanna.

▲▲▲▲▲▲▲▲▲▲▲

If he rode with his back to the sun
he reversed his bandanna to protect his neck.

When the sun became too hot,
the cowboy dipped his bandanna
into water, then put it under his hat.

Even when snow covered the ground
the cowboy worked.
He tied his bandanna over his eyes
to prevent snow blindness.

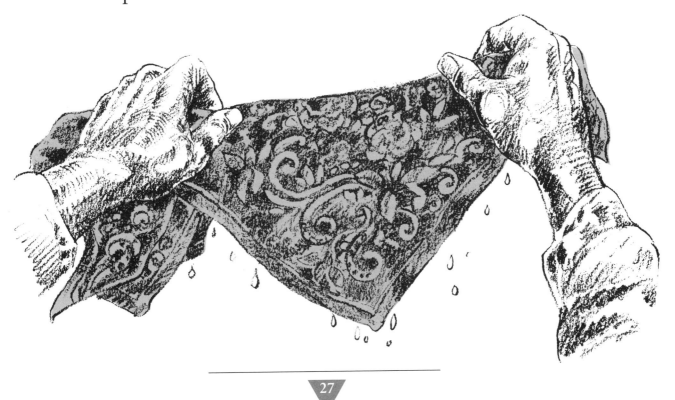

And he saved his ears from frostbite
by tying his hat brim over his ears.
With his bandanna tied under his chin,
he had instant earmuffs.

The cowboy liked having his "towel"
hanging around his neck after washing up for chow.
And if his plate was too hot to handle,
he had a handy pot holder.

On the trail his bandanna became a bandage
if he was injured.
And it hobbled his horse when he had no corral.

▲▲▲▲▲▲▲▲▲▲▲

Ask a cowboy why he wore a red or blue bandanna.

He has a ready answer:

"No need to rile a steer or a rustler with fancy colors.

Besides, that's the only colors the general store carries!"

4

THE SHIRT AND VEST

The prairie might be blistering hot by day
But when the sun set, the temperature dropped rapidly.
It would have been good to climb into a bunk
or a warm bedroll.

But the cowboy's day didn't end with the sunshine.
Rustlers, wolves, and changeable weather
made cattle restless.
Each man took his two-hour watch every night.

A cowboy who had worked up a sweat all day
might become dangerously chilled.

But he chose a shirt that helped protect him.
Made of heavy cotton or wool, it was suited
to the changing temperatures.
Its long sleeves kept out the wind, cold, and sun.

▲▲▲▲▲▲▲▲▲▲▲

And he wore sleeve garters of elastic webbing
or braided wires to hold his sleeves close to his arms,
for a loose sleeve was likely to catch on brush,
a low limb, or the saddle horn.

He chose dull colors for his shirt
because he believed that cattle and horses
might be afraid of bright ones.

▲▲▲▲▲▲▲▲▲▲▲

It was his vest that distinguished the cowboy.
He wanted something sleeveless and snug
that wouldn't snag on the saddle or underbrush.
When buttoned at night the vest held in his body heat.
By day it was unbuttoned and cool.

Mainly he wanted pockets-someplace to store his
tobacco, papers, matches, and his notebook.

His notebook just fit into his vest pocket.
A gift from the cattle commission, it held reminders
of special brands, the hours he had worked,
and how much money the boss owed him.

5

△△△△△△△△△△

THE PANTS AND CHAPARRERAS

In cattle country mesquite bushes and prickly cactus reached out to grab a man, it seemed.

And a raging steer with a lariat over his head could thrash and give the cowboy a rope burn.

Even at the ranch, a stubborn horse might tear open a man's leg on barbed wire fence.

The cowboy needed protection from these hazards.
For a long time, he had only loose-fitting woolen
or cotton trousers.
He was forever patching his pants-and his skin.

Around 1850 Levi Strauss made pants of tent canvas,
then denim, that were tough enough
to endure California gold mining.

The cowboy quickly adapted them for himself.
He bought them extra tight so that no loose ends
could be snagged on scrub.

They were so tight that a belt was unnecessary.
In fact, they were so tight that the pockets were useless.
But the cowboy wanted to get the feel of the saddle
beneath him.

Tough pants were fine for ordinary work.
But for extra protection the cowboy used "chaparreras."
They shortened the name to "chaps."

A waist-to-ankle leather apron, the chaps were split
up the middle.
They were tied with thongs at the waist and knees.

▲▲▲▲▲▲▲▲▲▲▲

In the north chaps were made of animal skins.
The cowboy called them "hair pants."

They were warm.
But in rain or mud they absorbed enough water
to make them heavy and smelly.

Another version was the batwing, made of leather
with winglike flaps.

But in Texas brush country the cowboy had little use
for the wing version.
He didn't want to give the brush anything extra to snag.
Slim and straight,
his chaps resembled a double-barreled shotgun.

When work was done the cowboy removed his chaps.
They were heavy and uncomfortable,
and they tended to slide down his narrow hips.

6

▲▲▲▲▲▲▲▲▲▲▲

THE BOOTS

The cowboy preferred to stay on his horse.
He gathered wood by lassoing it and hauling it up.
And he leaned over to open the corral gate.

He would gladly do any job
that didn't require him to dismount.
But sometimes there was nothing to do
but set foot on the ground.

Perhaps he had to climb down a steep embankment
to rescue a calf.
Then he would dig in his heels
and use his own body as a brace for his horse.

Spring thaws brought mud bogs,
and a few curious steers always became stuck.
As a bog rider the cowboy had to brace himself
to pull the steer loose,
or become helplessly trapped himself.
His high-heeled boots were good brakes for those jobs.

On horseback the cowboy was in constant danger.
Any moment his horse could shy and throw him.
If his foot hung in the saddle, he might be crushed
or stomped.
The cowboy needed footwear that would easily shake
loose from the stirrup.

The western boot looked fancy and decorative.
But no other piece of wearing apparel
made so much difference between life and death
on the range.

Each feature was designed to function on the job
and to guarantee its wearer's safety.

Once the western boot was introduced, around 1875,
the cowboy refused to buy the flat-heeled farm boots
found in the general store.

Instead, he stood on a piece of paper, traced his foot,
and measured his instep.
Then he sent his order and two month's pay
to a far-off bootmaker and waited.
It was six months before his boots arrived in town.
And it might be even longer before they caught up to him
on a trail drive.

The boot was most comfortable and practical
when the cowboy was in the saddle.
The seventeen-inch-high top kept out dust and gravel
kicked up by the horse.
And all the fancy stitching had a purpose, too.
It stiffened the tops so they didn't go limp
as the leather wore thin.

The boot had a thin insole
so the cowboy could feel the stirrup.

The toes were narrow and pointed
so that the cowboy could find the stirrup
of a restless, skittery horse in a hurry.
And they were stiff to protect his toes
from being trampled by cattle or by his own horse.

▲▲▲▲▲▲▲▲▲▲▲

That high, sloping heel was the real lifesaver.
It provided leverage on the ground.

And it kept his foot from slipping through the stirrup.
If he was thrown, the slope of the heel helped him
slip from the stirrup.

His boots were a source of pride to the cowboy.
He wore them skintight.
Mule ears-straps on each side-helped him
to pull them on.

And if they shrank from stomping through creeks,
he might stretch them by packing them with soaked oats.
Or he might just squeeze his poor feet into them
with grease and flour or soap.
Once his feet grew accustomed to the boot,
no other footgear was possible.

In town the cowboy appeared to swagger.
But that was the best he could do in his custom-made,
hand-tooled foot cripplers.

7

▲▲▲▲▲▲▲▲▲▲

THE EXTRAS

You could tell when a trail ride hit town
by the jingling sounds.

To the easterner the spurs seemed more decorative
than essential.
But the cowboy needed them in his daily routine.

Before he wore the spurs he filed down the points
on the star.
He didn't want to hurt his horse.

Although he called them his "pet makers,"
he used the spurs to encourage quick action by his mount.

The spurs touched to a horse's side quickened his pace.
They were held on by a leather shield over the instep
and chains beneath the instep.

His gloves, although they may have been embroidered
or fringed, were a necessity, too.

A rearing horse or a thrashing steer
could inflict rope burn.

His gloves, in addition to protecting him against injury
kept out frostbite and rain.

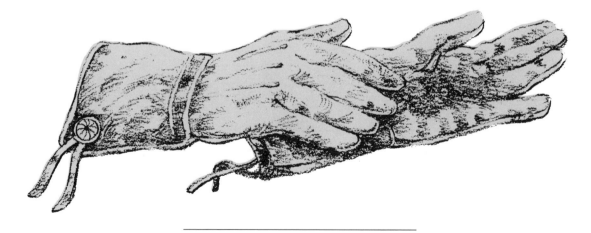

And no cowboy rode off without his "fish."
His yellow oilskin slicker was rolled and tied
behind his saddle.

He slipped it over his head
and it covered him from saddle horn to cantle
-the flared saddle back-in wet weather.

Its shine and rustling sound
could shy a nervous horse, though.

The cowboy carried a knife and a gun.

The knife could skewer a piece of meat from a hot skillet
or dig a stone from his horse's hoof.

The gun protected against rustlers, raiders,
and attacking animals.
But mostly it was a handy noisemaker to slow a
stampede or to make cattle move faster.
And it was used to kill incurably sick or injured animals.

On the trail the cowboy slept in a bedroll.
It was a water-shedding tarp
lined with quilts, blankets, or clothes.

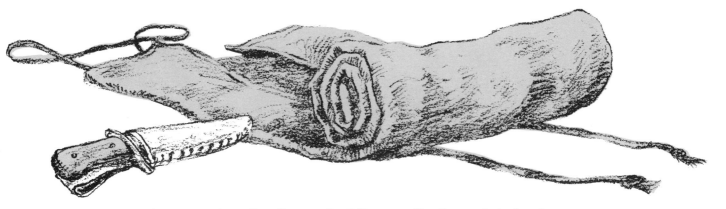

Each morning he "spooled," or rolled up, his bed,
tied it, and put it in the bedroll wagon.
If he traveled alone he carried it and cooking utensils
on a packhorse or mule.

The cowboy may have shared a comb on the trail,
but his bedroll was very personal.
He kept his money and few possessions rolled inside.

He didn't take kindly to anyone who
fooled around his "flea trap."

The cowboy worked hard and long.
He endured bad weather and loneliness.
Rarely did he have room or time for anything
that wasn't for his safety or convenience.

8

▲▲▲▲▲▲▲▲▲▲▲

THE HORSE: THE OTHER HALF OF THE COWBOY

The moon was hidden behind a bank of clouds.
The night was as sooty black
as the bottom of the chuck wagon pots.

The cowboy rocked back and forth in the saddle
as his horse slowly circled the herd.

Tired from sixteen hours' work, the cowboy dozed.
Suddenly he was jolted as his horse surged forward.
He squinted into the dark, seeing nothing.

It was up to his horse.
He had to trust it to avoid the prairie dog holes
he could not see.

In the darkness a cow had strayed from the herd.
The horse instinctively went after her.

This horse was a night horse, one with special talents.
It needed keen eyesight, gentleness,
and surefootedness.
The night horse, too, had a good sense of direction.
It could find camp again no matter where
the night adventures had led.

Each cowboy had between seven and ten horses.
He had a morning horse and an afternoon horse,
several half-trained horses,
and some horses selected for their special talents.

When there was branding or doctoring to be done,
the cowboy used his cutting horse to separate
an animal from the herd.

The cutting horse approached an animal quietly,
then spooked it at just the right moment.
The cow would bolt away, then dodge and spin,
trying to return to the herd.
But the cutting horse matched the cow's moves.

The job of the roping horse
was to stay at the side of a running cow.
A rope whizzing past its ears didn't bother this horse.

If the rope went slack, the horse dropped back.
It knew the rider had missed with the rope.

But if the rope caught its mark,
this horse instantly braced to halt the cow.
Its feet stood firm.
It pulled backward to keep the rope taut.
The cow couldn't move until the cowboy released her.

Especially important to the cowboy was
his river, or swimming, horse.

Trail drives crossed many rivers.
Frightened cattle could easily drown.
Or they might flow with the current
and stumble up the banks far downstream.

The cowboy needed a horse that
did not fear deep, rushing water.

▲▲▲▲▲▲▲▲▲▲▲

The horse was truly the other half of the cowboy.
He had to trust his life to his horse.

Nowadays the cattle are driven to market by truck.
The cowboy may ride fence in a low-flying plane.

But the horse remains an important asset on every ranch.
His ability to help the cowboy
in cutting and roping and climbing steep rocky land
is still unmatched by machine.

And the cowboy's costume,
so practically designed more than a hundred years ago,
is almost unchanged today.

ABOUT THE AUTHOR

"Riding the salt grass trail" on assignment for the *Houston Post* some years ago taught Mary Blount Christian something about the rigors of cowboy life. "Slicker that I was," she says, "I was ill prepared and was blistered by sun and saddle. The regular ranch hands had better equipment for the job—the bandanna alone convinced me that everything had a function." She made up her mind to write a book someday that would tell why the cowboy dressed the way he did. She titled that book *Hats Are for Watering Horses.* Ms. Christian's more than 100 published books for children include fiction and non-fiction. She is the author of *Hats off to John Stetson!, Who'd Believe John Colter?,* and *Sebastian (Super Sleuth).*

She is familiar with the land of boots and saddles and calls Houston, Texas, home.

ABOUT THE ILLUSTRATOR

Lyle Leo Miller has illustrated many children's books. He and his wife, a graphic designer, operate Flying Colors Studio in Dallas. He says, "Edie and I are frustrated ranchers. Our favorite part of the State Fair is the livestock. We took our toddler to her first Fat Stock Show in Fort Worth this year. This book will help her appreciate her heritage when she's older."

Lyle's grandfather Leo Miller was in the Oklahoma Land Run, and horses were used on the Miller farm until the forties. "Illustrating *Hats Are For Watering Horses* was a privilege for me—a chance to pay homage to the cowboy."